FEB 12

A Day in the Life: Grassland Animals

Baboon

Louise Spilsbury

Heinemann
LIBRARY

Chicago, Illinois

www.heinemannraintree.com
Visit our website to find out more information about Heinemann-Raintree books.

To order:

☎ Phone 888-454-2279

💻 Visit www.heinemannraintree.com to browse our catalog and order online.

Edited by Dan Nunn, Rebecca Rissman, Catherine Veitch, and Nancy Dickmann
Designed by Philippa Jenkins
Picture research by Mica Brancic
Originated by Capstone Global Library
Printed and bound in China by South China Printing Company Ltd

14 13 12 11 10
10 9 8 7 6 5 4 3 2 1

Library of Congress Cataloging-in-Publication Data
Spilsbury, Louise.
   Baboon / Louise Spilsbury.
     p. cm. — (A day in the life. Grassland animals)
   Includes bibliographical references and index.
   ISBN 978-1-4329-4727-9 (hc) — ISBN 978-1-4329-4737-8
(pb) 1. Baboons—Juvenile literature. I. Title.
   QL737.P93S65 2011
   599.8′65—dc22   2010017836

Acknowledgments
We would like to thank the following for permission to reproduce photographs: Alamy pp. 6 (© Ulrich Doering), 17 (© Photoshot Holdings Ltd), 18, 23 male (© Paul Springett 01), 22 (© Arco Images GmbH); Corbis p. 5 (© Craig Lovell); Getty p. 19 (Time & Life Pictures/John Dominis); Photolibrary p. 21 (Tips Italia); Shutterstock pp. 4 (© urosr), 8 (© Dennis Donohue), 9, 23 grassland (© Xtreme safari Inc.), 10, 23 grooming (© Jurie Maree), 11 (© Gert Johannes Jacobus Very), 12 (© Neil Bradfield), 13 (© EcoPrint), 14 (Igor Alyukov), 15, 23 communicate (© dwphotos), 16 (© ShutterVision), 20 (© Chris Kruger), 23 cliff (© Caitlin Mirra), 23 hyena (© Antonio Jorge Nunes), 23 insect (kd2).

Cover photograph of a chacma baboon in South Africa reproduced with permission of Shutterstock (© Chris Kruger). Back cover photographs of (left) a baboon's snout reproduced with permission of Alamy (© Ulrich Doering) and (right) baboons grooming reproduced with permission of Shutterstock (© Jurie Maree).

We would like to thank Michael Bright for his invaluable help in the preparation of this book.

The author would like to dedicate this book to her nephew and niece, Ben and Amelie: "I wrote these books for animal lovers like you. I hope you enjoy them". Aunty Louise.

Every effort has been made to contact copyright holders of material reproduced in this book. Any omissions will be rectified in subsequent printings if notice is given to the publisher.

All the Internet addresses (URLs) given in this book were valid at the time of going to press. However, due to the dynamic nature of the Internet, some addresses may have changed, or sites may have changed or ceased to exist since publication. While the author and publisher regret any inconvenience this may cause readers, no responsibility for any such changes can be accepted by either the author or the publisher.

Contents

Some words are in bold, **like this**. You can find out what they mean by looking in the glossary.

What Is a Baboon?

A baboon is a type of monkey.

Baboons are some of the biggest monkeys in the world!

Baboons live in groups of about 50 animals.

Baboons stay together in a group most days and nights.

What Do Baboons Look Like?

snout

A baboon has big ears, a snout, and small eyes.

It moves around on all fours and can climb trees well.

There are five different types of baboons.

All baboons look similar, but they have different colored hair.

Where Do Baboons Live?

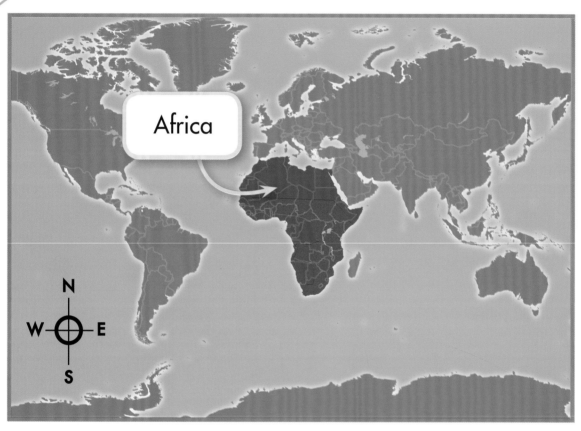

key: = where baboons live

Most baboons live in central and southern Africa.

They mostly live in places called **grasslands**.

In these grasslands, the land is covered in grasses and a few trees.

Mostly it is hot and dry, but in some months it rains a lot.

What Do Baboons Do During the Day?

Most baboons start the day by **grooming** each other.

They pick dirt and **insects** from each other's hair to keep clean.

After grooming, baboons start to look
for food.

At midday when it gets very hot, they rest
in a shady spot.

What Do Baboons Eat and Drink?

Baboons eat mostly grasses and other plants.

They sometimes eat small monkeys, spiders, frogs, and insects.

Baboons get some of the water they need from their food.

In the rainy months they drink from pools of water, too.

How Do Baboons Communicate?

Baboons **communicate** in different ways across wide **grassland** spaces.

They bark, grunt, roar, and chatter!

Baboons also communicate by smiling or showing their teeth.

By showing its teeth, a baboon warns other baboons it is ready to fight.

What Are Baboon Babies Like?

Baboon babies have black hair that gets lighter as they grow.

At first, the babies stay with their mother, day and night.

Later, young baboons play with each other in the day.

During play times they learn how to run, climb, and fight.

Which Animals Hunt Baboons?

During the day, animals like leopards, lions, and **hyenas** hunt baboons.

Some **male** baboons climb trees to watch for danger.

If a baboon spots danger, it barks.

The other males attack the dangerous animal or chase it away.

What Do Baboons Do at Night?

Baboons usually find a different place to sleep every night.

Before they sleep, baboons **groom** each other again.

Baboons climb up **cliffs** or high trees before it gets dark.

They sleep safely here because animals like lions cannot reach them.

Baboon Body Map

head

eye

tail

ear

snout

arm

leg

Glossary

 **cliff** high rock with a very steep side

 **communicate** give information or messages to others

 **grassland** land where mostly grasses grow

 **grooming** when animals clean each other's skin and hair

 **hyena** wild animal that mostly lives in grasslands in Africa. It looks like a dog.

 **insect** small animal with six legs. Ants, beetles, and bees are insects.

 **male** animal that can become a father when it is grown up

Find Out More

Books

Stewart, Melissa. *Baboons (Nature Watch)*. Minneapolis, MN: Lerner, 2006.

Taylor, Barbara. *Apes and Monkeys (Science Kids)*. New York: Kingfisher, 2007.

Walden, Katherine. *Baboons (Safari Animals)*. New York: PowerKids Press, 2009.

Websites

http://animals.nationalgeographic.com/animals/mammals/baboon/

http://www.bbc.co.uk/nature/species/Olive_Baboon

Index